Mandolin
Chord Book

by James Major

EXCLUSIVELY DISTRIBUTED BY

HAL•LEONARD®

CONTENTS

The Bonne Amie Musical Circle
circa. 1904 Milwaukee, Wis.

HOW TO USE THIS BOOK

This book is different than any other mandolin chord book in that the chords are arranged in keys. This enables you to find the chords most often found in any given key without having to flip through the whole book. For instance, in the key of C, C, F, G, and Am, are often found. These, and other related chords are all grouped together for easy reference. This enables you to find the most used chords in a key with just the turn of a page.

The shape of this book is also special. With it's slim design it fits into most mandolin cases, so you can take it with you to use as a convenient reference.

READING THE
CHORD DIAGRAMS

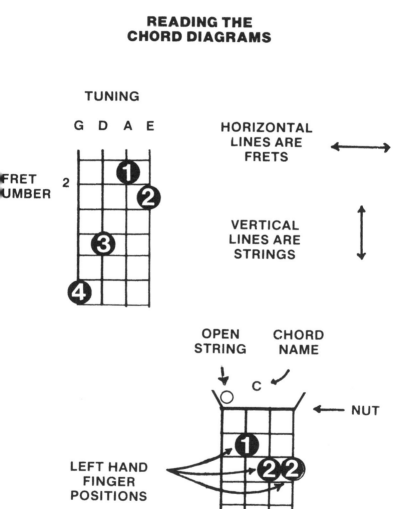

TUNING

G   D   A   E

FRET NUMBER   2

HORIZONTAL LINES ARE FRETS

VERTICAL LINES ARE STRINGS

OPEN STRING   CHORD NAME

C

NUT

LEFT HAND FINGER POSITIONS

1 = INDEX
2 = MIDDLE
3 = RING
4 = PINKY

3

A NOTE ON MANDOLINS

The mandolin family coincides with the violin family in that each member has a counterpart which is tuned the same as the other. The mandolin and the violin are tuned G, D, A, E. The tenor mandola is tuned the same as the viola C, G, D, A.

Flatiron mandola
scale length - 16$\frac{7}{8}$ in.

Givens mandolin
scale length - 13$\frac{7}{8}$ in.

Kundert viola
scale length - 14$\frac{13}{16}$ in.

Kundert violin
scale length - 12$\frac{7}{8}$ in.

The mando-cello (which is played on the lap like a guitar) and the cello are both tuned an octave below the tenor mandola C, G, D, A. The string bass and mando-bass also share the same tuning E, A, D, G.

Lyon & Healy mando-cello
scale length - 25⅞ in.

G. B. Gabbrielli 1769 cello
scale length - 27 in.

Gibson mando-bass
scale length - 42½ in.

Pfretchner string bass
scale length - 42 in.

A   A   A

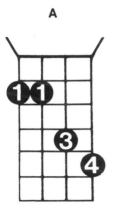 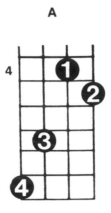 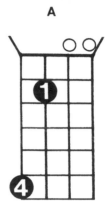

A7   A7   A△7

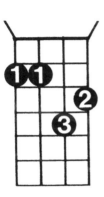 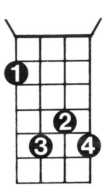 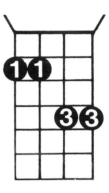

A6   Asus4   A9

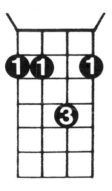 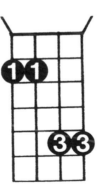 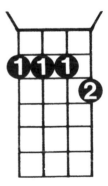

A aug   A dim   A7♭5

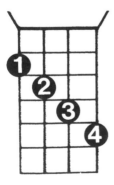 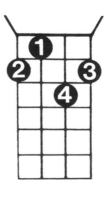 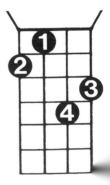

B

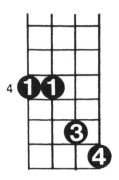

Bm

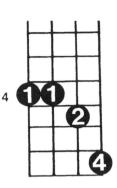

B7

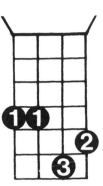

Bm7

C#

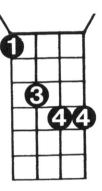

C#m

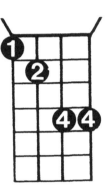

C#7

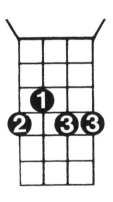

C#m7

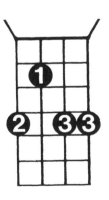

D

D

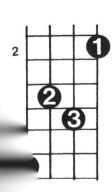

D△7

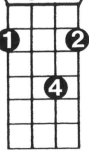

D6

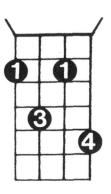

E7
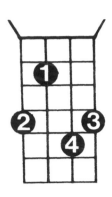

E
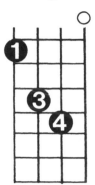

4

E△7
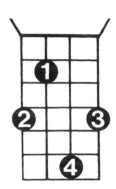

E9
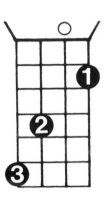

F#m

F#m
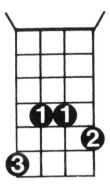

F#m
6

F#m7

F#7

F#
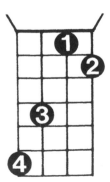

F#m6
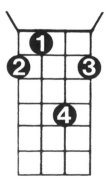

G#m7♭5
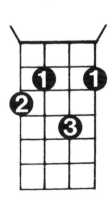

B♭ 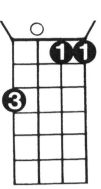 B♭ 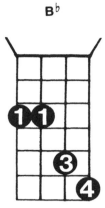 B♭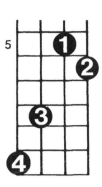

B♭7 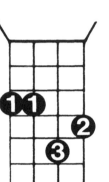 B♭7 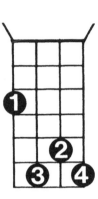 B♭△7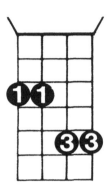

B♭6 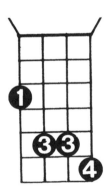 B♭9  B♭sus4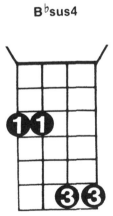

B♭aug 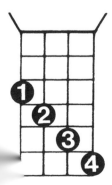 B♭dim 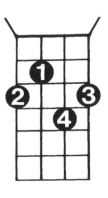 B♭7 ♭5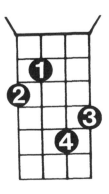

C

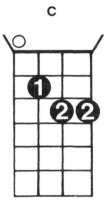

Cm

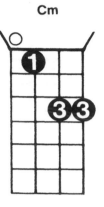

C7

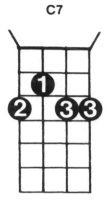

Cm7

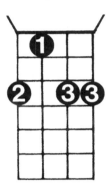

D

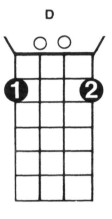

Dm

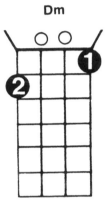

D7

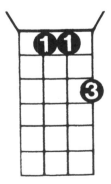

Dm7

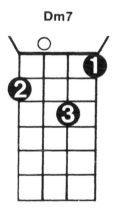

E♭

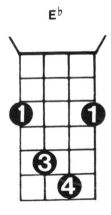

E♭

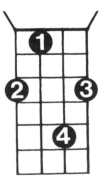

E♭△7

E♭9

F

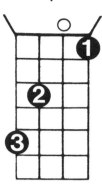

F7

F△7

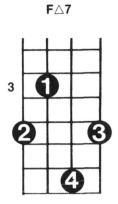

F6

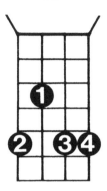

G

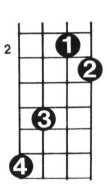

Gm

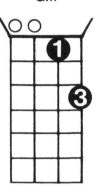

Gm

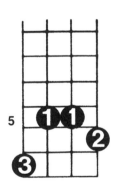

Gm

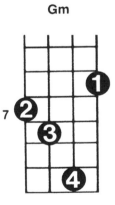

G7

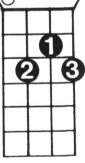

Gm7

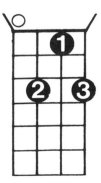

Gm6

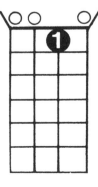

Am7♭5

11

B

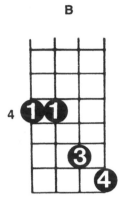

B

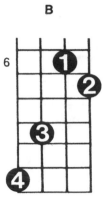

B

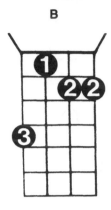

B7

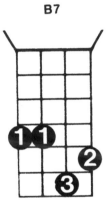

B7

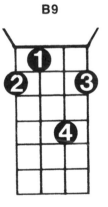

B△7

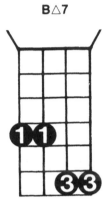

B6

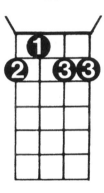

B9

Bsus4

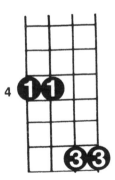

Bsus4

B aug

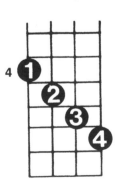

B dim

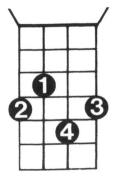

C#

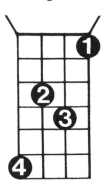

C#m

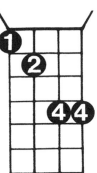

C#7

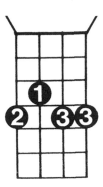

C#m7

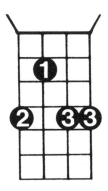

D#

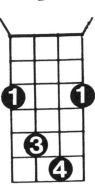

D#m

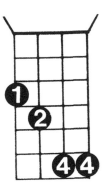

D#7

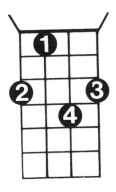

D#m7

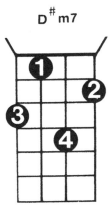

E

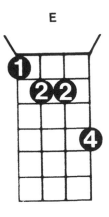

E

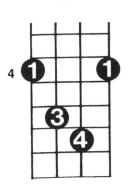

E△7

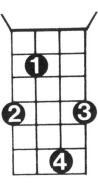

E6

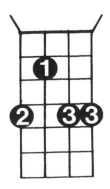

F#
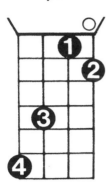

F#

F#7

F#9
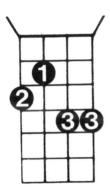

G#m
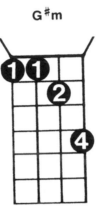

G#m
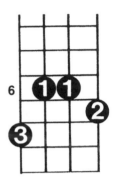

G#m
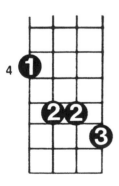

G#7

G#
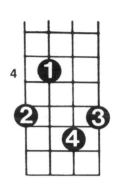

G#m7
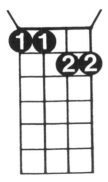

G#m6
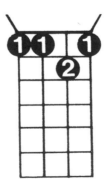

A#m7♭5

C

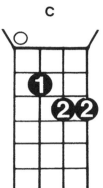

C

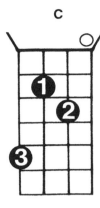

C

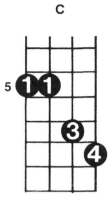

C7

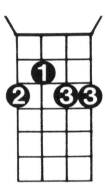

C7

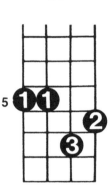

C6

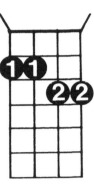

C△7

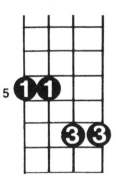

C9

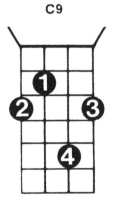

Csus4

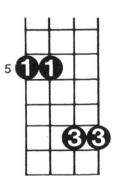

Csus4

C aug

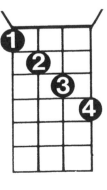

C dim

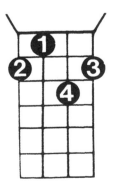

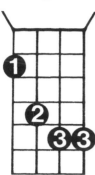
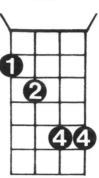
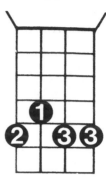

D   Dm   D7

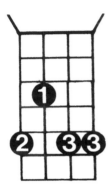
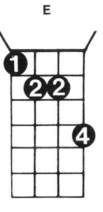

Dm7   E   Em

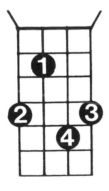
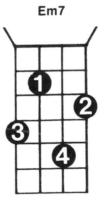
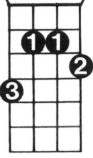

E7   Em7   F

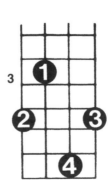
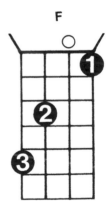

F   F△7   F6

G

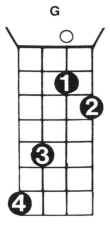

G

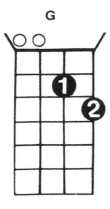

G7

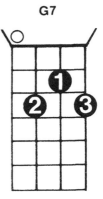

G9

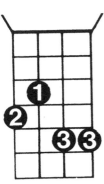

Am

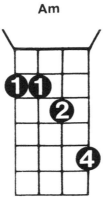

Am

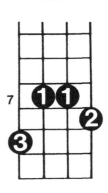

Am

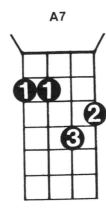

A7

A

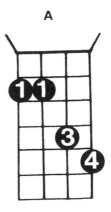

Am7

Am6

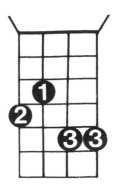

Bm7♭5

D♭

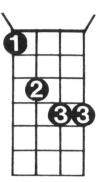

D♭

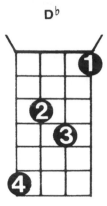

D♭

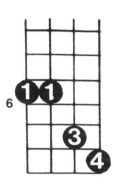

6

D♭7

D♭7

D♭△7

D♭6

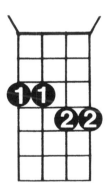

D♭9

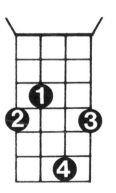

D♭sus4

D♭sus4

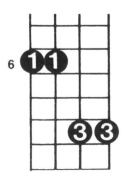

6

D♭aug

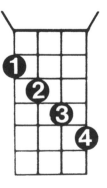

D♭dim

18

Chords For The
Key of D♭ and B♭m

E♭

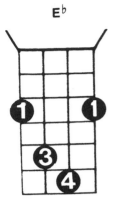

E♭m

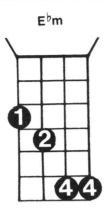

E♭7

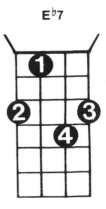

E♭m7

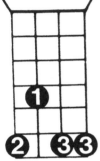

F

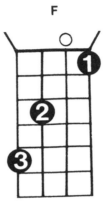

Fm

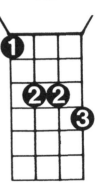

F7

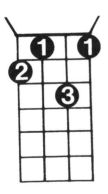

Fm7

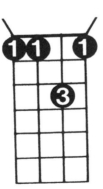

G♭

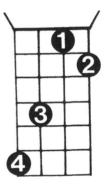

G♭

G♭△7

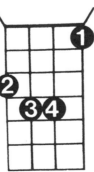

G♭6

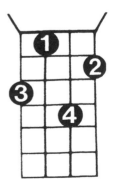

19

Chords For The
Key of D♭ and B♭m

A♭

A♭
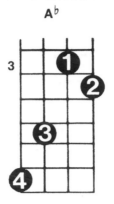

A♭7
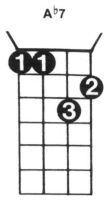

A♭9

B♭m

B♭m
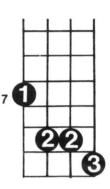

B♭m
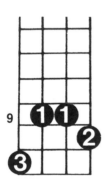

B♭
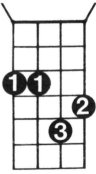

B♭7
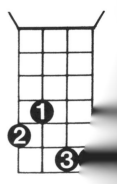

B♭m7
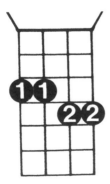

B♭m6
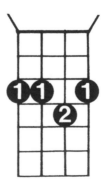

Cm7♭5

D

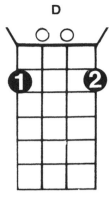

D

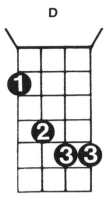

D

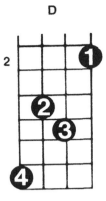

D7

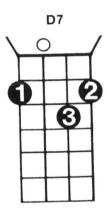

D7

D△7

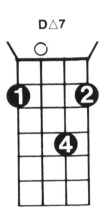

D6

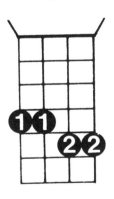

D9

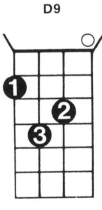

Dsus4

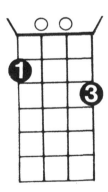

Dsus4

D aug

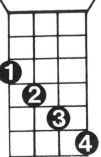

D dim

E

Em

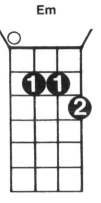

E7

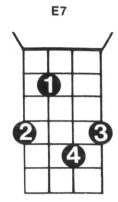

Em7

F#

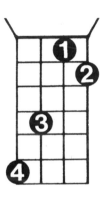

F#m

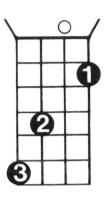

F#7

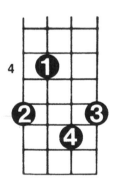

F#m7

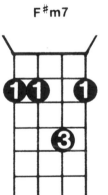

G

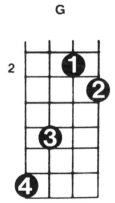

G

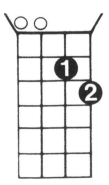

G△7

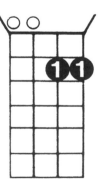

G6

Chords For The
Key of D and Bm

A
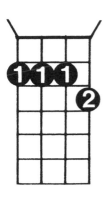

A
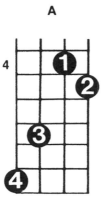

A7
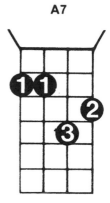

A9
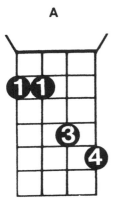

Bm
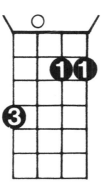

Bm
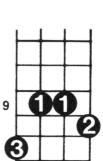

Bm
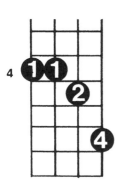

B
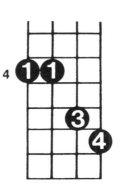

B7
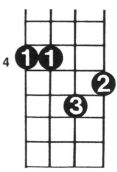

Bm7

Bm6
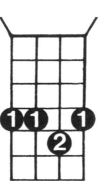

C#m7♭5
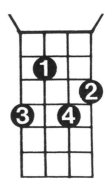

23

E♭

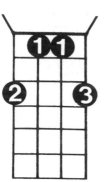

E♭

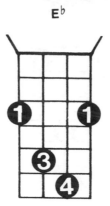

E♭

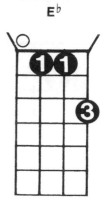

E♭7

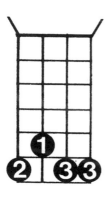

E♭7

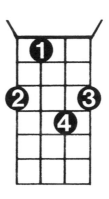

E♭△7

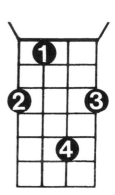

E♭6

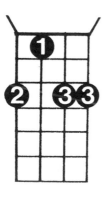

E♭9

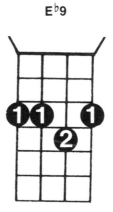

E♭sus4

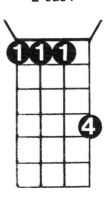

E♭sus4

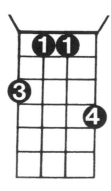

E♭aug

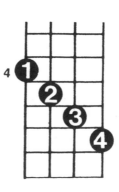

E♭dim

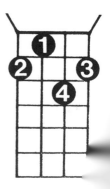

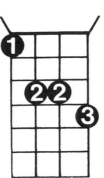

F

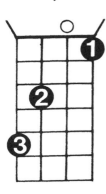

Fm

F7

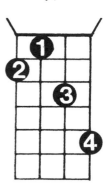

Fm7

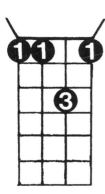

G

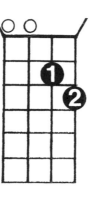

Gm

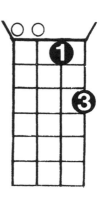

G7

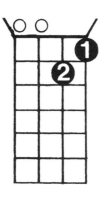

Gm7

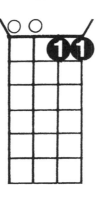

A♭

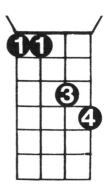

A♭

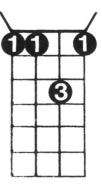

A♭△7

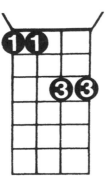

A♭6

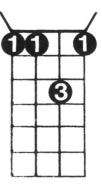

B♭ 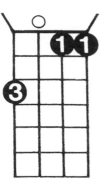 B♭ 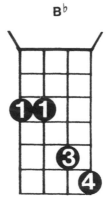 B♭7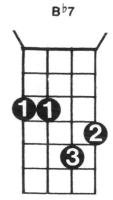

B♭9 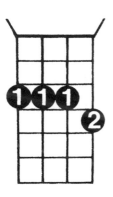 C 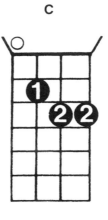 Cm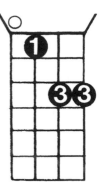

Cm 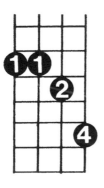 Cm 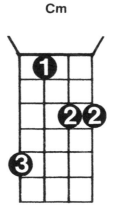 C7

Cm7  Cm6 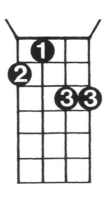 Dm7♭5

E

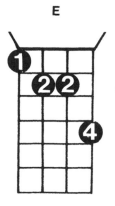

E

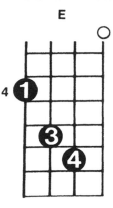

E

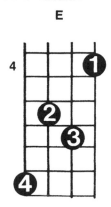

E7

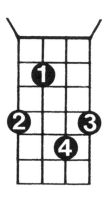

E7

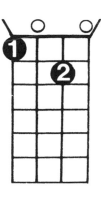

E△7

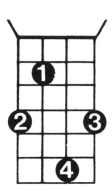

E6

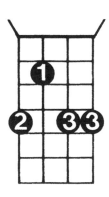

E9

Esus4

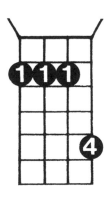

Esus4

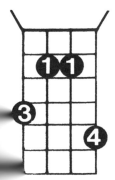

E aug

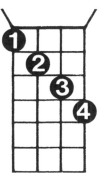

E dim

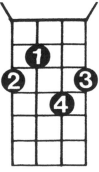

F#

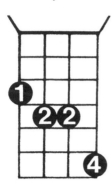

F#m

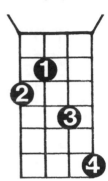

F#7

F#m7

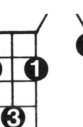

G#

G#m

G#7

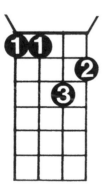

G#m7

A

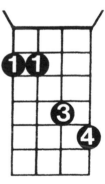

A

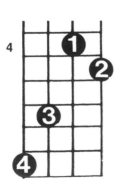

A△7

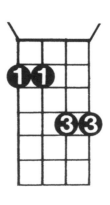

A6

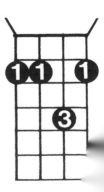

B   **B**   **B**

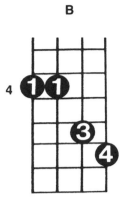
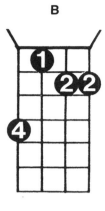

B9   **C#**   **C#m**

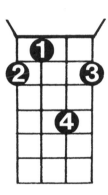
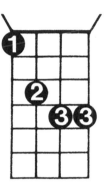
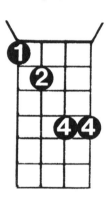

C#m   **C#m**   **C#7**

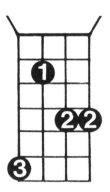
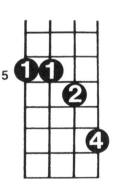
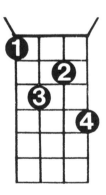

C#m7   **C#m6**   **D#m7♭5**

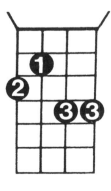
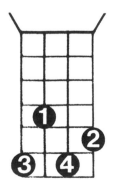

F

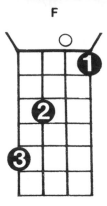

F

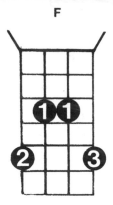

F

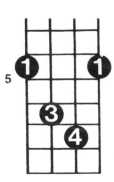

F7

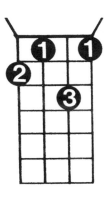

F7

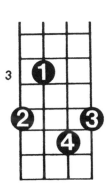

F△7

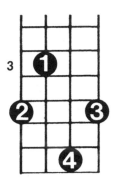

F6

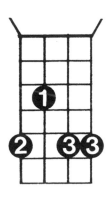

F9

Fsus4

Fsus4

F aug

F dim

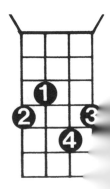

G

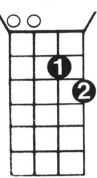

Gm

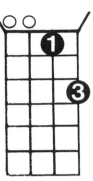

G7

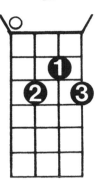

Gm7

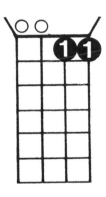

A

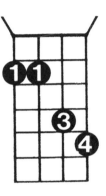

Am

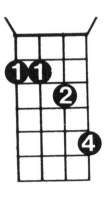

A7

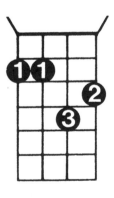

Am7

B$^\flat$

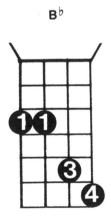

B$^\flat$

B$^\flat\triangle$7

B$^\flat$6

C

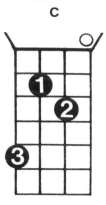

C

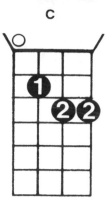

C7

C9

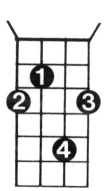

D

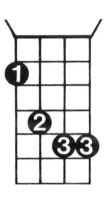

Dm

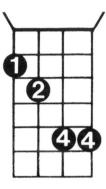

Dm

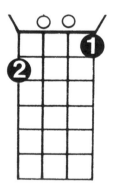

Dm

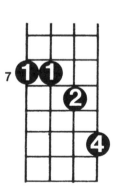

D7

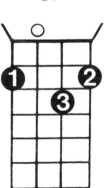

Dm7

Dm6

Em7♭5

G♭
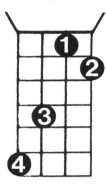

G♭
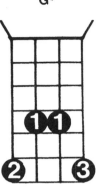

G♭
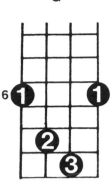

G♭7
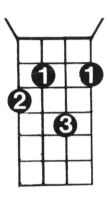

G♭7
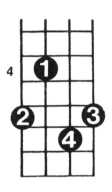

G♭△7
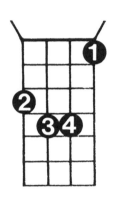

G♭6
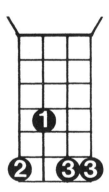

G♭9

G♭sus4
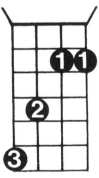

G♭sus4
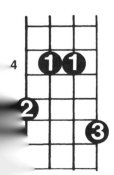

G♭aug
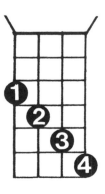

G♭dim
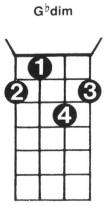

33

Chords For The
Key of G♭ and E♭m

A♭

A♭m
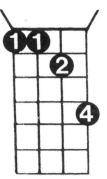

A♭7
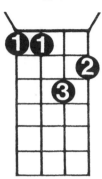

A♭m7

B♭
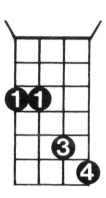

B♭m
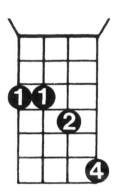

B♭7
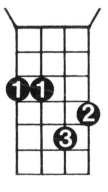

B♭m7
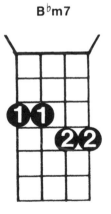

B
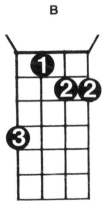

B
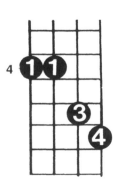

B△7

B6

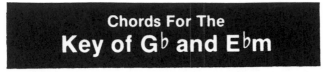

Chords For The
Key of G♭ and E♭m

D♭

D♭

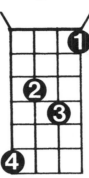

D♭7

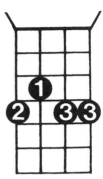

D♭9

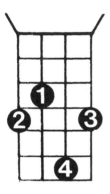

E♭

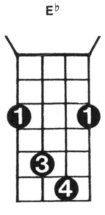

E♭m

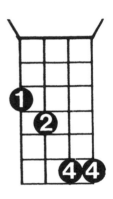

E♭m

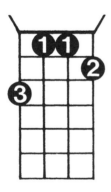

E♭m

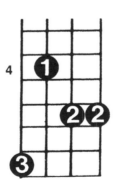

E♭7

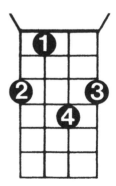

E♭m7

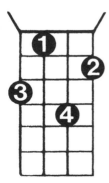

E♭m6

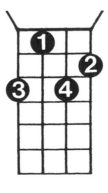

Fm7♭5

G

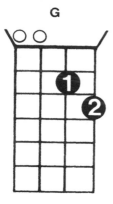

G

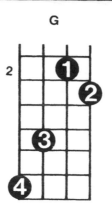

G

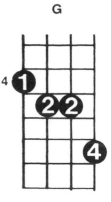

G7

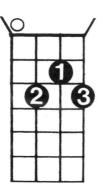

G7

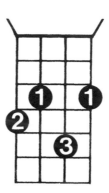

G△7

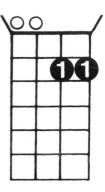

G6

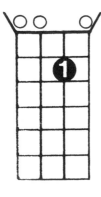

G9

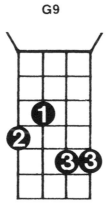

Gsus4

Gsus4

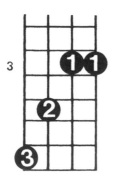

G dim

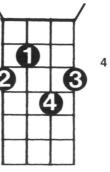

G aug

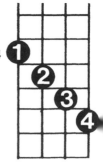

A
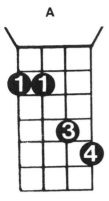

Am
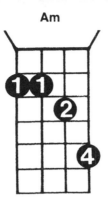

A7
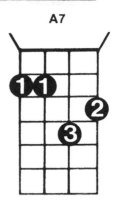

Am7
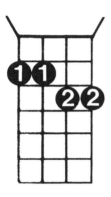

B
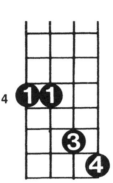

Bm
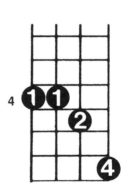

B7
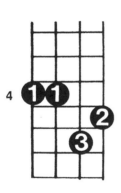

Bm7
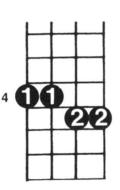

C

C
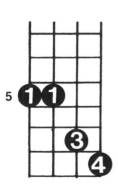

C△7
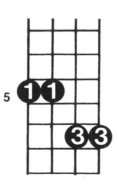

C6
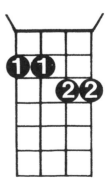

D
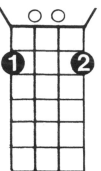

D
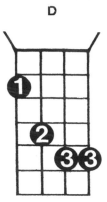

D7

D9
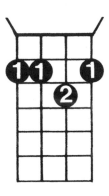

E
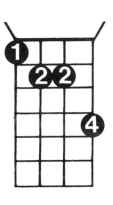

Em
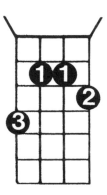

Em
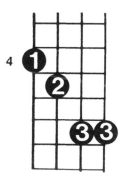

Em
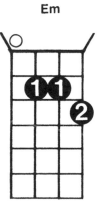

E7
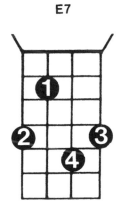

Em7
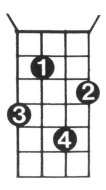

Em6
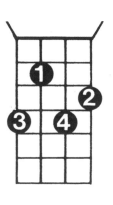

F#m7♭5
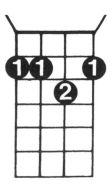

A♭

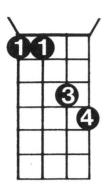

A♭

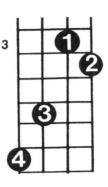

A♭

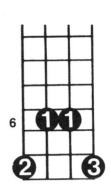

A♭7

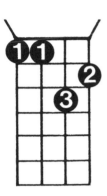

A♭7

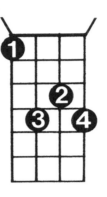

A♭△7

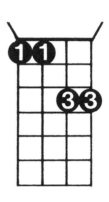

A♭6

A♭9

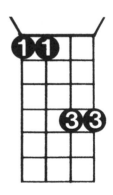

A♭sus4

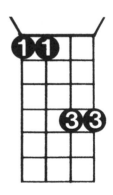

A♭sus4

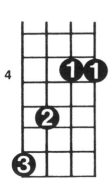

A♭aug

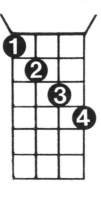

A♭dim

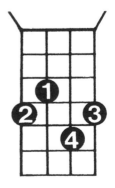

B♭

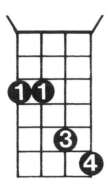

B♭m

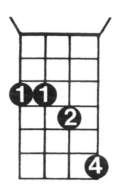

B♭7

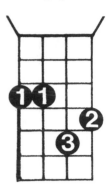

B♭m7

C

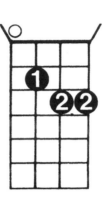

Cm

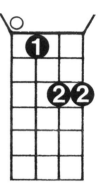

C7

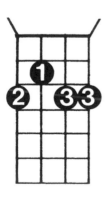

Cm7

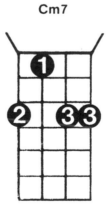

D♭

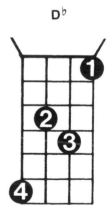

D♭

D♭△7

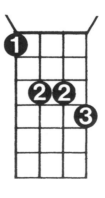

D♭6

40

E♭

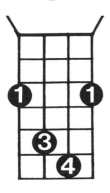

E♭

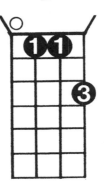

E♭7

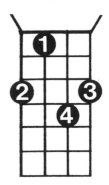

E♭9

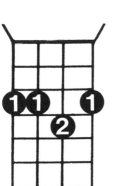

F

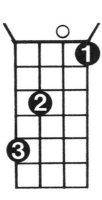

Fm

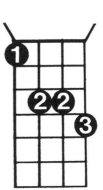

Fm

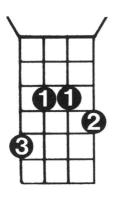

Fm

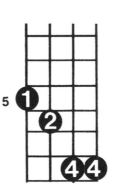

F7

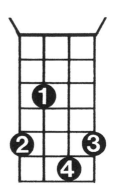

Fm7

Fm6

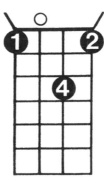

Gm7♭5

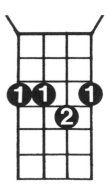